The story you are about to read is the true account of the author, in her own words. To preserve the authenticity of the story, little editing was done.

To my husband Bruce of twenty-nine years and all the individuals who helped us heal and recover from our devastating loss when Kodi left this world. We truly love and appreciate all the love and support that was shown to us in our time of need by all our family and friends.

My Little Kodi Bug

That kiss was the last one my baby would receive from me while she was still alive.

Patti Jo Wheeler

Published by W.H.Wax Publishing, LLC.

My Little Kodi Bug
Written by
Patti Jo Wheeler
© 2023 Patti Jo Wheeler
whwaxpublishing.com/pattijowheeler

Photography By
Kelsie Richardson
KR Photography
whwaxpublishing.com/kelsierichardson

Editing by
Casandra Chadwick
W.H.Wax Publishing, LLC.
casi.chadwick@whwaxpublishing.com

Published by
W.H.Wax Publishing, LLC.
619 County Road 249
Jordan, Arkansas 72519
info@whwaxpublishing.com
whwaxpublishing.com

Library of Congress Control Number: 2023932325

ISBN (paperback): 9781662936951

Proudly printed in the United States of America

The Story of My Little Kodi Bug

July 16 to 19, 2001 I had to be in Springdale, Arkansas for a training class with a company I work for in Grannis, Arkansas. I have a hard time going on these company training trips because it takes time away from my family and from the little girl that took me five years to conceive.

I have four children, Kris my fourteen-year-old son, Kasey my eleven-year-old daughter, Emily my eleven-year-old stepdaughter, and Kodi my ten-month-old little girl. As you can see from the gap in the ages of my children Kodi was born after a lot of thought and time.

I wanted to have a baby so badly, for five very long years. On August 31, 2000, I was blessed with a precious little angel from above. To my absolute despair, having her here would only last ten months and nineteen days.

When I returned home on Thursday evening from Springdale, I longed to see Kodi. But she wasn't there, my babysitter still had her in the town of Mena, Arkansas.

My babysitter finally brought her home around 6:30 p.m. We played around and I loved on her until it was around 9:30 p.m. At that time, I decided to try to put her to sleep because I had to work the next day.

Kodi didn't want to go to sleep, she wanted to continue playing. She loved to act like she was attacking me by biting on my chin and making a growling sound. It was so cute! But she started getting teeth that wasn't so pleasant, that night I let her do it anyway.

The night was passing fast, and she still didn't want to go to sleep. So, I asked my husband to try and rock her to sleep. Kodi never went to sleep unless she was rocked. I wanted it that way because I am a working mom who doesn't get to see her child during the day. Kodi went to her daddy that night so I could go to bed. My husband rocked her, but she fussed a little. I stood in the hall listening, in a place I knew she couldn't see me. I wanted to go back in the living room and get her, but I knew she didn't want to go to sleep. So, when she stopped fussing, I went on to bed.

If I would have only known that was the last time I would ever be able to rock my child to sleep again, I never would of went to bed.

During the night Kodi woke up, it was around 3:00 a.m. I went to her room and got her and took her to my bedroom to finish out the night with us. She immediately went right back to sleep, no bottle, no nothing. She only wanted to be with her mommy and daddy. This was also always done because I just wanted to be around her all the time. While she was asleep, while she was awake. It didn't matter, just so she was near.

Even when I went to church, I couldn't put her in the nursery because I wanted her to be with me. No matter how wiggly or fussy she got in church, she was staying with me.

Friday morning, I woke up at my normal time of 5:00 a.m. to get ready for work. Kodi and my husband stayed asleep the whole time I was getting ready for work.

When it was time for me to leave, I put my daughter's daily supplies in the car. After that, I went to my bedroom and picked Kodi up from the bed where she laid. I took her straight to the car and put her in the car seat. While driving to the babysitter I kept looking in the rearview mirror at her sleepy little eyes closing and opening. She is so cute, is what my mind would think, how lucky I am!

When I got to the babysitter's house, I carried Kodi and her supplies to the door. That day my babysitter was hard to wake up, or so I thought. The doorbell didn't work. When I knocked, she answered. Before I left, I kissed Kodi on the head and told her that I loved her. She was still so sleepy from me waking her so early.

That kiss was the last one my baby would receive from me while she was still alive.

Thinking back, you always say if I would have done this, or that, or whatever. But it doesn't change anything, nor could it.

I went on to work at my job in Grannis. I have pictures of Kodi all over my office. That day all I concentrated on was work cause I needed to catch up from being away on the training trip.

At 2:30 p.m. Friday, July 20, 2001, I had to leave work to go to Mena, Arkansas, which is about thirty-five minutes from work, to pick up trophies for my daughter Kasey's softball team.

I stopped by my house first to tell my husband where I was going and to see if my son Kris wanted to go with me. He decided to go.

Something in my mind said, go pick up Kodi before you go to Mena. I thought about it for a second and something even stronger said, no, wait and pick her up when you get back.

Over and over, I thought of this. So, I decided to

listen to what I thought was my brain at the time. But later realized my Heavenly Father didn't want me to go through what he knew I couldn't handle.

Kris and I went to Mena, finished our business, and were heading back to Grannis. We were right outside of the city limits when a cop, traveling really fast pulled up behind my car and made us stop.

I thought maybe I was speeding. I had no idea my life was about to change with the words he would speak.

He came running up to my window and said,

"Are you Patti Wheeler?" I said, "Yes." "Patti, one of your children is being transported to DeQueen hospital by ambulance."

I screamed, "WHICH ONE?!"

When I said it, I knew which one it was because my son was with me, and my daughter Kasey was in Texas with my sister. The cop replied, "I don't know."

I screamed, "NOT THE BABY!! OH MY GOD, NOT THE BABY!!" I threw my face into my hands and started crying and I couldn't stop.

The police officer said, "Can you drive to DeQueen?" At first, I said, "NO!" Then when I looked in his face it was like looking at somebody thinking, now what do I do? So, I said, "Yes, I can drive," and started to pull back onto the highway. Leaving the policeman standing by the side of the road, I drove like a mad person.

Our highways are so dangerous that at normal speeds it is very possible to have a wreck. Well, God was with me on that drive from Mena to DeQueen. It took me about thirty-five minutes to drive a fifty-to-fifty-five-minute drive. I was passing people on curves and hills at about eighty miles per hour. My son was with me, and he was scared to death.

The whole way I was honking and flashing my lights, nobody wanted to pull over and let me through.

So, as you might guess, they moved out of my way because I was a crazy woman on a mission to reach my daughter and no one was going to slow me down.

I have one of those stupid car phones that has a hard time getting a signal to call out with. My son didn't know how to use the car phone, so during my daredevil driving, I was also trying to call anyone who could tell me what was happening. I finally reached my mom's work answering machine.

I screamed in the phone, "GET OFF THE PHONE! WHAT'S WRONG WITH KODI?! GET OFF THE PHONE!"

I hung up with that machine and called my sister's house. I finally reached a human, but I wish now that I wouldn't of. My niece Whitney answered the phone at my sister's house. I was screaming when I talked to her.

I yelled into the phone, "WHITNEY! WHAT'S WRONG WITH KODI?!"

Whitney was crying and said to me, "Aunt Patti, Kodi is not breathing. They took her to the hospital." I said, "WHAT?!"

As you might imagine, my phone lost connection.

So now, here is this crazy woman behind the wheel of a car driving eighty miles per hour on curves and hills, knowing that her little angel was no longer breathing.

God was with us, protecting us and every car that I met on that highway.

I finally reached the hospital. It seemed like it took hours. I squealed into the parking lot and jumped out.

My family was already there at the hospital. My sister Michelle, who has a hard time thinking before she speaks, said as I was running up to them,

"She is still not breathing."

I didn't even make it to the place they were standing when she said that I dropped to my knees. My family came to where I was and helped me inside to the waiting room.

As you can probably imagine, I had a very hard time waiting. I wanted to know something, and I wanted to know right now!

I was praying and crying and praying and crying. Begging God to let my little girl live.

The room we waited in wasn't far from where my little darling was being worked on.

The room they were in was silent. I knew in my heart she was gone. They were too quiet.

Minutes later the doctor appeared in the waiting room and said the words that would tear my heart and soul into a million pieces that no one could fix.

"I'm sorry, the little baby didn't make it. She died."

I started screaming at the top of my lungs,

"NO! NO! NO!"

I lost control. I was hitting things and people. I didn't want anyone to touch me. How could this happen? She was fine this morning. This is not real. Not my baby!

A nurse settled me down and asked, "Do you want to see her?" I said, "Yes."

Walking into where she laid was the most incredible agony I had ever experienced. She laid there with her eyes closed and tubes in her mouth. Blood was on her little shirt.

How could this be?

I kissed her lips and her head and held her hand and hugged her. From this point on it would be too hard for me to tell you the rest of what happened in the hospital. It was a turn for the worst.

We left when the Arkansas State Coroner came and picked Kodi up. I would not leave, not until then. They came about three hours after I had got there.

My friend's husband drove me and my husband back to our house in Grannis.

I wanted to die and didn't care who knew it. I wanted to be with my little child on her journey.

My husband kept telling me that the other children needed me here. At that time, I didn't care what they needed. I needed to die so I could be buried with my little angel.

I don't really remember very much of the next three days. The medicine I was on had me knocked out most of the time.

On the third day, the police came to our home. They told us that our daughter suffered a blow to the back of her head that caused her to die.

They asked us questions about what happened that morning and that night before. They also asked my husband if he had hit her. I couldn't believe what I was hearing. I had thought that Kodi died from SIDS while taking her afternoon nap at the babysitter's house.

When this news of how Kodi died was given to us, my feelings changed dramatically.

I was angry at my babysitter. How could she have let this happen? Did she do it? Did one of the children at her house do it? What happened to her? These are a few of the many questions I asked myself continuously throughout the days.

So many people were at our house the next week that it was hard to rest or to grieve. Everyone was so mad and confused about what was happening to us. The day before my daughter's funeral she was returned to DeQueen funeral home.

The funeral home called us and told us she would be ready to be seen around 9:00 a.m. I wanted to go see her, but I didn't if you can understand that.

When we got there my stomach was so tore up. To this point, I still had not eaten and was still being forced to drink.

When I walked into that room my heart sank. My little angel was lying in that little coffin. My mind screamed, WHY?! WHY?! I went and kneeled beside her and started to cry and pray. I touched her and kissed her and hugged her. I loved her so much. She looked like she was just sleeping and if I stayed long enough, she would wake up and we could go home together.

If I kissed and hugged her enough and if I ran my fingers over her hair, would she wake up for me?

I promised my little girl I would find out who had done this to her as I kissed her little face for the last time that day.

I went home from that place with my heart in my hands. My heart was smashed, and my tears would not stop. My mind would go back to when I dropped her off that dreadful day of July 20, 2001.

On the day of my daughter's funeral, while driving to the funeral home, I was looking out the window and my mind was seeing my little angel running on the hillside beside our car. Everywhere I looked, there she was, running right alongside us. Finally, the pain of seeing her made me close my eyes until we reached the place we were going.

The funeral lasted too long for me. The songs tore at my heartstrings, and the pain was too much. How could I handle this pain?

It was my turn to say goodbye to my daughter for the last time. The last time I would actually see her precious little face.

I kneeled beside her once again. My mind kept saying, this is not happening, I am not here. That is not my child laying there. It couldn't be, I waited too long to get pregnant with her. I did everything the way I was supposed to. I rocked her to sleep at night, I spoiled her every way that I could. She was my little angel. Why did she have to go?

I didn't want to leave her side. I wanted to go with her. I wanted to die right then so I could go, but it didn't happen. Life on this earth is so cruel. I didn't want my daughter to go, and she did anyway. When I desperately wanted to go, I couldn't.

I kissed and hugged my little Kodi Bug for the last time. This moment is burned into my heart, my body, and my soul.

The drive to where my daughter would be laid to rest seemed so short. I could no longer keep my eyes open, even though I had refused to take medicine on this day. It was the last time I would see her, and I didn't want to forget it.

At the cemetery, I could no longer walk, talk, or keep my body in an upright position. When it was time to go home my husband helped carry me to the car. When we got to our house, he picked me up, carried me into the house, and laid me on our bed.

The second my head hit the pillow I was asleep. I didn't dream. I didn't do anything but go into a deep, deep, sleep. I have never slept that way in my life.

I truly believe that God put me to sleep because I went through all that my soul and spirit could handle. I have heard that nothing is put on you that you can't handle. I believe that is a true statement. When it gets too hard, God steps in and takes care of you. I didn't realize how many people were praying for me and my family.

I slept for three hours and then woke up to a feeling of peace. A peace that I had never felt in my life. But then life kicked in again, and not too long after I awoke, that feeling left. I think it left because of all the negative people around me.

This day seemed to last a long time. When night came only a few people remained. There were about eleven people here, most of us were outside under the carport, but some remained inside at the kitchen table. My phone rang and my sister answered it.

Now, for what I am about to tell you, you can believe it or not, it is up to you. But I know God was at work in a powerful way.

When my sister Michelle answered the phone the person on the other end of the line was my other sister April. She lives in Texas with her family, but she was here for our family crisis. April was at Michelle's house in Gillham, about six miles from where my house is in Grannis.

April was talking to Michelle about some things that had just happened where she was. She told Michelle that about thirty minutes ago her daughter Kendra, who is four years old, asked her, "Momma, will you pray and ask God if Kodi can come and play with me?"

April said she wasn't sure what to tell Kendra. But this is what she told her, "Honey, Kodi is with God, and I don't think she is allowed to come and play with you."

Kendra accepted that answer and returned to watching cartoons with her little brother and her cousin Gavin. About five minutes had passed and the phone rang. The caller ID did not list a phone number so Gavin told April, "Don't answer it cause we don't answer it if we don't know who is calling."

April decided she would answer it anyway. She picked up the phone and said, "Hello? Hello? Hello?" but no one would respond to her, so she hung the phone up.

At that time, Kendra became upset with her mother and said, "Momma, that was Kodi on the phone, and the reason she couldn't say anything is because she is a baby."

April said her mouth dropped open and she just looked at Kendra in dismay. Then she told her that she didn't think it was Kodi. Kendra insisted that it was too her on the other end of that phone. So, my sister decided to just drop it and leave it alone. Everyone settled back in again and returned to watching the cartoons that were playing on the television set.

About fifteen minutes later, Kendra turned around, looked into April's eyes, and as serious as she could, asked her, "Momma, can I tell you something?" April replied, "Yes honey, you can tell me anything."

Kendra said without hesitation, "Kodi is sitting behind you Momma."

At that point, I'm sure you can imagine the look on my sister's face when she heard those words. April said without thinking she looked behind herself to see if Kodi was there.

April exclaimed, "Kendra, what did you say?!"

Kendra, not knowing that she was upsetting April, once again said, "Kodi is sitting right behind you Momma."

April, without thinking, jumped from the couch and looked at the spot where she had been sitting.

With panic in her voice and fear on her face said, "Kendra, where is she now?"

Kendra pointed toward the ceiling of the living room and said to her mother, "She is right there on the ceiling Momma."

April, completely frantic and dismayed, had to call an adult. This is the conversation my two sisters had on the phone while I was outside with some of my friends and family.

My mother was sitting at the kitchen table watching Michelle's face as it lit up and a smile stretched from ear to ear. She was listening to the events that had unfolded with Kendra and April. When Michelle finished listening to all the things April had to say, she hung up the phone and proceeded to tell my mother exactly what she was told. After Michelle finished telling Mom what April said she immediately did what April had instructed them not to do.

Mom walked right up to me, kneeled beside the chair I was sitting in, and told me what had happened. I was a little confused about what she was telling me. As soon as Mom finished telling me, she walked inside the house.

I proceeded to tell everyone that was there what I was told. My husband just looked at me. Some of my friends and family that were sitting there said, "It can happen."

I asked my husband, "Do you want to call and talk to Kendra on the phone and see what she says about it?" He said he did want to talk to her and walked into the house, so I assumed he was going to call Kendra.

About five minutes later, I got up and went into the house to see what Kendra had told him. To my surprise, he had not called her yet. He said, "Patti, you call and talk to her." I picked up the phone and called Kendra. April answered the phone. We talked for just moments, and April said, "I told them not to tell you." I told her, "It's okay." I asked April, "Do you mind if I talk to Kendra?" April's reply was, "It's okay with me if it's alright with you."

When Kendra got on the phone, I said, "Kendra, did you see Kodi?" Her sweet little voice replied and said, "Yes Aunt Patti, I did." My heart sank. I thought maybe if she seen her once, she would see her again. So, I asked Kendra if she would do me a favor. The favor I asked her was this, "Kendra, if you see Kodi again, would you tell her I love her and miss her?"

Once I finished speaking there was a pause, and then I heard Kendra say, "Kodi, your Momma says she loves you and misses you."

My heart sank once again. I said, "Kendra, is Kodi still there with you?" Her reply was, "Yes, she is still here, and I told her what you told me to tell her."

Then she said something that really surprised me. She said, "There are two Kodis." Of course, you can imagine that when she said those words, I began to doubt what she had told me. I said, "There are two Kodis there with you?" Then Kendra, with a little chuckle said, "Wait a minute, there is only one Kodi, the other one is my sister."

I said, "Your sister?" She said, "Yes, it is my sister and Kodi." When she spoke those words I could hear April saying something in the background. Then, before I could speak, Kendra said, "Can I sing you a song, Aunt Patti?" I really wanted to talk to April right then but how could I refuse this request?

So, I listened to her sing me a little song. When she was finished I told her it was a beautiful song. She was so happy I said that. She finally let me talk to April. Once on the phone, April said, "I never told her, I never told her."

What April was talking about was that she had a miscarriage when Kendra was around one and a half years old. So, we believe that it was indeed Kendra's sister that was with Kodi.

The night was not over for the miracles that were happening.

I got off the phone with April and told everyone that was still at my house about my conversation with Kendra. Everyone was excited about what was happening. As the night went on, the men were sitting outside and the women were all inside, that is a very normal thing around here. But, for some reason, all the men got up and came inside with the women.

There were nine people here, four men, four women, and my eleven-year-old daughter Kasey...

... when the next thing happened.

We were all in the kitchen talking about what had happened at Michelle's house and the conversation I had with Kendra. Then the phone rang and for the first time since all this happened, not one person was talking.

My husband answered the phone and said, "Hello?" He pulled the phone from his ear slightly and looked at it then placed the phone back up to his ear and said, "Hello?" once again. After the second hello from my husband, the color of his face ran out, he was white as a sheet. He handed the phone to my mother and said, "You have to hear this."

My Mom placed the phone up to her ear and said, "Hello?" Her reaction was the same as my husband's. Mom then pulled the phone from her ear and said, "Everyone in the room needs to hear this." So, the phone was passed from one person to the other. Everyone said, "Hello" one time and then, with a look of confusion, pulled the phone from their ear and passed it to the next person. When the phone got to me I said, "Hello?"

What I heard was the sound of my own voice being transferred back into my own ear as if it had gone into a cavern and then came back out and was put into my ear. It was the weirdest thing I have ever heard in my life. I said "Hello" about five times. The word hello was not what my brain was telling me to say. My brain was telling me to say,

I love you Kodi, I miss you, sweetie. But all that came from my mouth was, "Hello?"

I felt a comfort come over me like I have never felt in my life. I too passed the phone to the next person beside me. It was my best friend, Teri. She said, "Hello?" one time and she also turned white as a sheet, just like my husband.

The phone went all the way around the room and returned to my mother, she said, "Hello?" for what would have been her second time and was disappointed to hear nothing. No return voice, no static, nothing at all. The phone was back to normal.

My husband got the phone from my mother and said, "Hello? Hello?" but there was nothing. So, he placed the phone back on the receiver. Everyone in the room was in a state of wonder.

My husband slipped out of the room and walked towards the bedroom. When he returned, I asked him where he had gone. He said, "Well, that's the way it happened with Kendra, so I went to Kodi's room to try and see her." I told Bruce that I believed only the pure at heart can see something like that and I didn't think this happened so he could see her. He was a little depressed by this. But he had his own little miracle earlier that day, and he hadn't even realized it.

This is what happened with Bruce.

When we got home from the funeral, Bruce placed me on the bed. He decided to change clothes so he could go to City Hall to eat with the rest of the family and friends that had been with us that day.

Bruce decided to wear a pair of new shorts I had bought him back in June. I bought these shorts for him when we went on vacation to San Antonio in June, but he never wore them. The shorts still had the tags on them and were lying on the dresser under some stuff in our bedroom.

I'm not a perfect housekeeper, so he had to do what I call "digging them out." Before he put them on, he pulled the tags off, then as he was straightening the pockets up and he felt what he thought was lint. But, as he was pulling out the lint, he found out it wasn't lint. It was a small budding flower. He was a little shocked by this but didn't think much about it, even though the flowers from the funeral had not come to the house yet. He decided to keep it.

I believe that little flower was from Kodi to her daddy.

After the phone call, and Bruce trying to see Kodi, Bruce picked up his little flower from the shelf he had set it on and told the group of friends and family about how he had gotten that flower. Everyone agreed that flower was meant for him.

The conversation about what had just happened with the phone was all we were talking about for the next hour or so. Then the phone rang again, but it was my sister April. We all wanted it to be Kodi again.

April said she had talked to Kendra just to see if she really saw Kodi. April said she asked Kendra, "Are you sure it was Kodi that you saw?" Kendra, being a little irritated that her mother could ask such a question, firmly stated, "Yes mother, it was Kodi, and you seen her too." April replied, "Kendra, you did not see Kodi." Kendra, being a bit more irritated by this, firmly stated again, "Yes mother, it was Kodi, and you seen her too, and she was wearing a yellow crown on her head."

April, after hearing this, decided to call and tell us what Kendra had said to her and to ask if the color yellow meant anything to us. The color yellow is the color that I loved seeing Kodi wear and the color of the clothes she was laid to rest in. April, being happy with that answer, hung up the phone.

Shortly after that conversation, April's husband returned to Michelle's house, so she came up to join us.

April said she just had to be where we were. There was too much excitement for her to stay away. By this time, it was getting pretty late.

As the conversation went on, my mother was in the process of telling me and Bruce that we loved Kodi so much and she loved us so much. About the time she finished saying the last word, an awful look came over her face. I thought she was having a heart attack. She was shaking and her eyes were as wide as they could be. She was hanging on to the arms of the chair with everything she had.

"Mom, are you alright?" She didn't answer me. I said it again, this time with her voice shaking, and with so much excitement in her tone, she said, "It felt as if I was being lifted from this chair. I thought I was floating up into the air and I couldn't stop. Everything from my toes to my head were tingling."

Now, I don't know exactly what happened to her cause it has never happened to me. But I have heard of some people getting touched by the Holy Spirit and I believe that was what happened to her. She was so happy after that happened. She could not control her excitement. I believe God works in many ways to help us in our time of need.

You could feel the presence of love and peace in the room.

That very night my heart changed.

I no longer wanted anyone to die for what had happened to my little Kodi Bug. I no longer felt the need for revenge against anyone. All I felt was peace and forgiveness.

Now, I'm not saying that I didn't need to know what really happened to my child, cause I still had to know that. But I felt that I was not alone anymore. I felt that someone would be holding my hand and helping me through this terrible time.

The night was growing very late. It was time for us to turn in for bed. So, we said our goodbyes to everyone. But before they left, my husband had this to say to them, "Don't tell anyone about this, they will think we are crazy." Everyone said their goodbyes and the remainder of the family, that was camped out here, said their good nights. Bruce and I went to bed.

My mom was the last one to turn in for the night. But before she was able to fall asleep, the phone rang again. Mom told me the next morning that she had been afraid to answer the phone because she was alone, but she did anyway. It was April again.

April told Mom that when she had returned to Michelle's house, that Kendra was still awake, so she asked her Again, "Kendra, are you sure it was Kodi that you seen?" Kendra said to her mother, "Yes momma, it was Kodi, and her fingernails were painted pink."

April was very surprised by this because Kendra had not seen Kodi at all. If you are wondering if they indeed were pink, yes, they were painted the brightest pink you have ever seen. The babysitter painted them about three days before this happened.

Now, whether you believe this or not is up to you. I know what happened... I was there, and so were the other eight people. April and Kendra were also involved in this event.

I will never forget what happened and will never forget how our Heavenly Father helped me when I needed him the most.

Now I will tell you how my life changed after this happened. But, before I can do that, I have to tell you a little about the path I was on before.

I hardly ever went to church, maybe once a month, every other month or so, but only on Sundays from 11:00 til noon. I had so much to do that I didn't feel I had time to go any more than that, and really, I didn't want to.

I prayed the same prayer every single night, you know the one.

"Dear Heavenly Father, thank you for all the things you have done for me today. Thank you for keeping my children safe. Thank you for watching over us. Jesus' name, Amen."

Sound familiar?

I wasn't baptized or saved. You could say I was going about my daily life any way that I wanted to. Now, that is not saying I was doing anything to break the law or anything. I just wasn't living for God.

August 31, 2001

The day that would have been my daughter's first birthday. I couldn't go to work; it was a depressing day. I wanted to go see my daughter at the cemetery. But for some reason, I just kept putting it off and putting it off.

Around 7:00 p.m. that night I decided it was time. So, I went to the cemetery, and I talked to Kodi and told her how much I loved and missed her. I was there about an hour when my babysitter and her friend pulled up. My heart sank. I had not spoken to her or seen her since the morning I dropped Kodi off for the last time.

My heart started beating and I started shaking. I was in a state of thinking, what do I do now?

Something inside of me said... it will be okay. As Ronda proceeded to get out of the car all I could do was continue staring at the mound of flowers lying on the ground. As she approached, I looked up to see the tears in her eyes, the swollen puffy eyes that indicated she had been crying for quite some time. She spoke the first words I had heard her say in over a month.

"Can I give this to her? I made it for her birthday." I nodded my head, yes. Ronda placed the little white satin cross with the flower down close to the head of the grave that read, "Happy 1st Birthday Kodi Bug". I was just looking at her as I knelt beside the foot of the grave.

Ronda walked over to where I was kneeling and knelt beside me. I turned my head to where I was facing her and asked her the question that had bothered me for so long.

"Why didn't you call me?" She told me she didn't know what to say. We talked for about an hour. As we talked, we cried and held each other in our time of grief. I don't know if you think this was a big step or not, but it was for me.

This is the woman that I wanted to kill with my bare hands. This is the woman I wanted to shoot with a gun. This is the woman who was responsible for caring for my daughter on the day she died.

Had God meant for us to meet on this very day, my daughter's birthday? Had God brought us together for a reason? I didn't know. But after all that God had given me, all I could do was tell her I forgave her. I truly do forgive her. I don't believe she had any control over what the devil had laid out to happen to my daughter.

My babysitter needs a lot of prayers to help her deal with what has happened. So, I am asking that you pray for her and her family and that she receives some relief from her grief.

As Ronda was leaving the cemetery, my husband and our neighbor were pulling up to where I was. Ronda left and I walked over to my husband's pick-up truck. The look on my husband's face was a look of disappointment. My husband thought that when I saw Ronda for the first time after all this had happened, that I would kill her. So, before he could ask me what had happened, I told him I forgave her. You could say he was not very pleased with me. See, during this month and eleven days we did a role reversal. I went from wanting to kill to forgiving, and he went from saying maybe they didn't know what happened, to wanting revenge. So, my husband and his family did not share in my forgiveness.

I have been hitting a brick wall since I told them I forgave her. I guess time and a lot of prayers will be the only thing that will help them forgive.

The church that I attended every once in a while, was having a revival. I decided I needed to go, even though facing all the people would be very hard for me to do. I decided if my mom, my sister, and my friend would go with me, I could do it.

Looking back, I think it was because of God that I was able to go. You see, not only is it the church I go to, but it is also the church my babysitter goes to. Even though I had already spoken with Ronda, I still wasn't real comfortable with it.

The last night of the revival was a Friday night. On this night everyone gave what you would call testimony.

As I sat there listening to different people express the feelings and changes that were going on inside them, I thought to myself, I need to say something.

As the last person went to sit down, I was so scared, I knew I wanted to say something to everyone. But what would I say?

The brother started to close the service so we could go to the meeting hall to eat before we went home. My words were on my tongue, and I was ready to speak. But as I was trying to get the brother's attention, he didn't seem to hear me. I guess you could say I was talking very low. So, he continued to speak about the closing. But my mother heard me, and she spoke up for me. She got the brother's attention very loudly and told him I had something to say.

So, as you might say, I had the floor. At work I have had to speak with groups of people, so you would think this would not be too difficult for me, but it was hard. I could not look up and I started to cry. Finally, the words I wanted to say started coming from my mouth.

This is what I wanted so desperately to say...

"I know everyone here knows what has happened to me recently. I want to thank every one of you for all the prayers that you have said for me and my family. Those prayers helped me so much. With all the prayers that you said, God started to help me and my family on the night of Kodi's funeral. Right after Kodi left us, I wanted to kill someone. I wanted revenge for what had happened. I wanted someone to pay for my grief. But the night of Kodi's funeral that all changed. I was so at peace that I couldn't believe it myself. All I could do was forgive the ones that hurt me so much. Thank you so much for all your prayers, God does answer prayers and I wanted to tell you that."

I believe that the Holy Spirit was with me talking to the church that night.

After the service, we went to the meeting hall to eat. Yes, my babysitter was there that night. After I finished eating, I went over to where my babysitter was sitting and asked her if she wanted to help me, and my family, decorate Kodi's resting place at 9:00 a.m. the next morning. She said that she did. I went back to where my family was sitting and told them what I had done. I can tell you; it went over like a ton of bricks, but they didn't put up a fight.

The next morning, I was the first to arrive at the cemetery, then Ronda showed up, followed by my family.

For the next few hours, we all worked on fixing the grave the way I wanted it to be. After we finished, Ronda took pictures of it. We all were just standing around, nobody really wanted to leave.

My mom started to walk to her car. The look on my mother's face was a look of sadness. So, before she could get to her car, I said wait, we need to say a prayer.

Everyone came up to the grave. I spoke up and said, "We all need to hold hands." Everyone circled around my daughter's resting place and held hands. I started to say a prayer to our Heavenly Father.

After the prayer was over, we opened our eyes, and it was so bright. My nephew Gavin said, "Who flashed the light?" Mom then said, "Did you see that dust stuff fly up?" All I noticed was that it was extremely bright, but they saw something. I don't know what it was, but whatever it was, I believe it was heavenly sent.

September the 30th, 2001, I was saved and baptized.

This is the story of what God has helped me through. You can believe me or not, it is totally up to you. I felt compelled to write what has happened to me and my family.

My little Kodi Bug is in Heaven with our Heavenly Father, waiting for the day we can join her. May everyone who reads this be as touched as I was when I went through it during those days!

May God bless you and keep you close to his heart.

Another Life

Seven years after my daughter's passing, my son Kristopher's English Teacher Mrs. Baar sent me an assignment he had turned in while in school. I wanted to share it with you.

The assignment is titled "Another Life."

If I could change or prevent one event in my past experience, I would choose to prevent the death of my youngest sister. Kodi Leah Wheeler was born on August 31st, 2000. My mother and stepfather have been married almost fifteen years now. In those fifteen years together, they have only been able to have one child. Kodi would be six years old this past August. It seems like so long ago, yet it feels like yesterday that we pulled up to the hospital to find out that she was gone. My mother was devastated to the point she thought about personal suicide after ending Kasey and my own life to be with Kodi. My stepfather does not talk about what happened, but we can all see the impact it had in his life. I feel like I could have changed this by watching my sister rather than her going to the babysitter's house that day. All our lives would be completely different if Kodi was still with us today. Mom would not cry anymore, and my stepfather might be more open. Kasey would have a little

sister to protect and talk to when she needed. I probably
would have made a lot better choices in high school. I could
have made better grades, hung out more with friends rather
than sitting at home and continued to play basketball like I
always wanted. I felt like I had to work so that my mom
would not have to worry about me as much. I know now
that my mom would have been fine with any choice I made.
We all know where Kodi is and that we will see her again.

Written By Kristopher Silzell
Mrs. Baar English Class.

My Peace Tested:

After Kodi's birthday, life went on whether I wanted it to or not. People went about their daily lives as if nothing had happened. It seemed as if I was in a sea of despair alone. Some days I would be fine, and others were tears after tears. I returned to work after approximately a month off. My husband said I no longer needed to stay home, I needed to return to the world. What??? I couldn't. I didn't belong there anymore. My only thoughts were what happened to my child? How could I even possibly think about work?

Through my hesitation, I returned to work. Sitting in my office, crying daily, not wanting to be there. I had only got this promotion about two weeks before Kodi passed. I no longer wanted this job. I no longer wanted this life. I still had my peace, but it would be tested.

September 11th, 2001, remember that day. I was at work, and everyone was glued to the TV for the events that were unfolding, watching the planes fly into the towers. As I watched them all sitting around the conference table, all I could think about was Kodi. I didn't want to watch more suffering. I lowered my head and returned to my office. I wanted no part of the madness that was unfolding on national TV.

For weeks all that was talked about was 911. I felt for everyone involved, but my grief was still so strong. I was barely holding on.

The autopsy on Kodi was performed, and the documents were with the state investigator. The cause of death was listed as a homicide. To say my emotions were all over the place would be an understatement.

The state investigator asked us to come and speak with him at his office in Mena. I barely recall the meeting with him. I was still on medication to control my overwhelming sense of loss and fear of this life.

When we got to his office, we were directed upstairs. My mind was on my daughter as we sat and listened to him talk about the investigation. He needed us to take a polygraph test, and they would be requiring one from the babysitter and her husband. I knew this man was trying to do his job, but I was in disbelief that he wanted us to take a polygraph test.

For reference, I dropped Kodi off at the babysitter's early that morning. She was fine when I left her. At three something in the afternoon is when the ambulance was called to the babysitter's house.

I had called the coroner's office myself, weeks prior, because I wanted to know what happened to my child. He told me he couldn't give me any details, but he could tell me that she didn't suffer. He believed she was injured around 11:00 a.m. and that once it happened, she never regained consciousness.

Did he not share that same information with the state investigators? I did speak up and told him what the coroner said to me, and he said, "Well, it is protocol that we give all involved a polygraph test."

Are you kidding me? She was injured at 11:00 a.m. at the babysitter's house. We were at work. The only people involved were the people at the babysitter's house.

We agreed to do the test. But I can honestly say that I did not like this man, nor did I want to be anywhere around him.

Our appointment was made to take the polygraph test.

We were told it had to be a month out and that we were not allowed to be on any medications. If we were on anti-depressants, we would need to stop them immediately. Neither my husband nor I were on any anti-depressants.

I was on medication that helped me calm down but now I had to stop them to do this test. I wanted to know what happened to my child, and if this is what it took, then I would do it.

My husband and I drove to Hope, Arkansas, and took the test. Now it was the babysitter's turn. She and her family passed the test that day. It wasn't until later that I found out from her husband that she never stopped taking her anti-depressants and that she was on medicine before Kodi passed.

To say I was floored would be an understatement.

What I didn't mention earlier in the story was that the evening before Kodi passed away, Ronda called me and said that she didn't want to babysit anymore, that she just couldn't do it anymore. The phone call didn't last a long time. I understood that sometimes people want to change what they're doing in their lives.

I asked Ronda if she could watch her Friday and over the weekend, I would find someone else. Even though she agreed to watch Kodi that next day, I asked my son Kris if he could watch his sister the next day and the typical teenage response was, "Mom, no, I don't want to watch her."

So, to Ronda's house, she would go for one last time. If I would have only known what was going to happen, I wouldn't of went to work. I would have quit. I would have never let anyone besides myself watch her again.

Right? That is the way our brains work when life slaps you in the face and knocks you down.

As hard as it was to live through all the trauma of our loss, we would have to continue. Our peace would continue to be tested over and over again.

The investigation continued. We made several attempts to find out what was going on with our daughters' case. The Sheriff's office was irritated that we called so much, that we wanted answers.

One day my husband and I decided to drive to Mena to speak with the Sheriff in person. During that conversation, I wanted to rip his head off.

It went like this. "Have you found out anything?" He replied, "No, we are working on it." "Did you do anything about the babysitter taking medication during her polygraph?" He replied, "No" and then added, "She is suffering, every time I speak with her you can tell she has been crying for days, I don't think we need to put anything else on her right now."

Are you kidding me? We lost our child, our light, and we don't need to put her through anything else? To say we were floored and pissed off would be putting it mildly.

Our conversation with him was getting heated. He told us what she had said in her statement to the police when they interviewed her. She had stated that she gave Kodi a bottle around 11:00 a.m. and laid her down on a mattress in front of the air conditioner to sleep. She then stated that her husband had come home, and she asked him to watch her and the other kids while she took a bath. She stated that while she was in the bath, her husband noticed that Kodi was no longer breathing, he yelled for her and told her. She stated they tried CPR and called 911. Later in her statement, she stated that her stepson, who has down-syndrome, may have gotten upset with Kodi due to Ronda laying her in his sitting spot where he watches TV on that mattress.

So, was she saying he did it? What was she saying? That she wasn't watching her very well and that he did something to her? The Sheriff said it could have happened.

Oh my gosh! I don't even know what to think or do.

I ended it by asking him to get my child's belongings from her house. I wanted her stuff back. I wanted all of it returned to me. Only a few things were returned about a month later.

Life proceeded to go on. Did I still have faith that God was helping me? Absolutely! Had God not been with me I wouldn't be here today telling Kodi's story. Does that mean that life was going to get easier? Nope.

Kodi passed in 2001, and my sister Michelle got pregnant in early 2002. My best friend Teri also got pregnant, and my husband's ex-wife also got pregnant. How in the world is this fair? So many people so close to me pregnant, blessed with a child, but mine was taken. How could I be happy for them? How could I live through this torment anymore? I wanted my child back. I wanted justice for her death. I wanted to know what happened. I didn't need to be reminded that it took me years to get pregnant with her, and she was only allowed to stay ten months and nineteen days.

Now I would have to endure the feelings of anger that would arise when baby showers were planned, and babies were born.

I felt as though I was turning into someone I didn't want to be, a person filled with anger and rage. A person who could not handle all this pressure. To ease the pain that was building inside of me, I wrote in my journal daily of what I was feeling and how I was being tested. I wrote of all the things wrong in my life. I wrote about how angry I was. I wrote about so much.

I needed my God to walk in front of me because I was breaking. Day by day, the peace was slipping away. All the wonderful things God had let us experience days after Kodi passed was slipping out of my hands and heart, being replaced by anger, rage, and jealousy. How could this be so? How could it all have been for nothing?

Time passed and babies were born. My niece Tommie was born in October of 2002. To say that she was the healing and help I needed was an understatement. I didn't know that when I was so angry at my sister, she was carrying the child that would once again restore hope and joy to my life. I needed that child more than I knew.

When my sister was pregnant, she asked me if Bruce and I wanted to adopt. It was a pregnancy she had not planned. To me, it felt like a blessing for her to ask. In my heart, I was so afraid that it would ruin our relationship. I didn't want that, even if it meant I wouldn't have a baby to love. My husband also said that if we adopted, we would no longer try to have any more. I wanted to have a baby of our own. So, I told my sister no.

But God has a way of working around all that. Tommie spent all her time with us. She was at our house every day. She spent her early childhood growing up at our house. She was just like our own. I cannot tell you the healing power of the smile of a little one. God knew what I needed, and he provided.

A year after Kodi passed, her death certificate was changed to an accident. No one was charged with her death. No one informed us that they were changing it to accidental. The only copy of the autopsy we have still has homicide on it.

Life is still rolling on. So many things have happened since that dreadful day. There is sadness, there is grief, and there are tears, still, every holiday, every birthday, and on random days when my mind wonders.

But there is hope. There is a God who provides. Through the years, I have had many friends lose children, and when I say I am praying for the Comforter to be with you and them, I mean it from the bottom of my heart. Without him, the road is too hard, and life is unbearable when you suffer such a great loss.

May his peace and comfort always be with you on good days and bad days.

In loving memory of Kodi Leah Wheeler (Bug)

Born August 31, 2000. Went to Heaven July 20, 2001

I can do all things through Christ who strengthens me.

Philippians 4:13

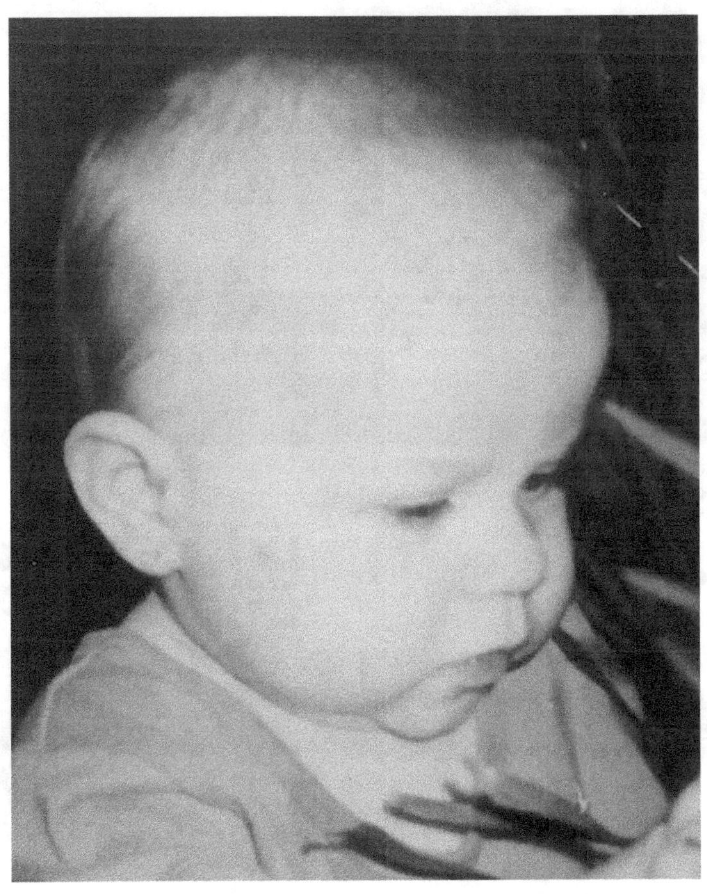

About the Author
Patti Jo Wheeler

Patti Jo currently resides on a small cattle farm near the town of Wickes in Southwest Arkansas with her husband Bruce, their thirteen-year-old son Korey, and their fourteen-year-old niece Kaden. Patti Jo and her sister, April Lambert, recently opened the successful Rise and Shine Café in Grannis, Arkansas. Patti Jo is a child loss survivor and mother to a rainbow child, Korey Fredrick Wheeler, born 2009.

To order
My Little Kodi Bug
Please follow the link below or scan the QR Code.

whwaxpublishing.com/pattijowheeler